MW00917188

30-Day

· ·

Prayer
Challenge

· ·

for Teen Girls

The
30-Day

....

Prayer
Challenge

....

for Teen Girls

Nicole O'Dell

BARBOUR BOOKS
An Imprint of Barbour Publishing, Inc.

Published by Barbour Books, an imprint of Barbour Publishing, Inc., 1810 Barbour Drive, Uhrichsville, Ohio 44683, www.barbourbooks.com

Our mission is to inspire the world with the life-changing message of the Bible.

Member of the
Evangelical Christian
Publishers Association

Printed in the United States of America.

INTRODUCTION

Welcome to *The 30-Day Prayer Challenge for Teen Girls*! This book will walk you through some tough issues and help you answer questions that all girls face. You are not alone with your doubts and confusion, so let's tackle them together.

After a daily reading that will help you see things the way God does, there are some questions to help you learn from your own thoughts and experiences about that topic. Do your best to be honest as you explore your answers because that's the only way to really grow. Your answers to those questions will help you apply the truth to your life. Then, three prayer focuses—morning, afternoon, and evening—will keep you thinking and praying about that topic all day so it will take root in your heart.

The thirty days of focus will show you how important and beneficial it is to be in the Word of God daily and how much of an impact regular prayer times will have on your life. Pay attention to how your attitudes and expectations are changed as you spend time with Jesus and how you begin to look forward to that time each day. Plan now to take those practices forward beyond these thirty days and make them a part of the rest of your life.

Day 1

MIND GAMES

*We demolish arguments and every pretension
that sets itself up against the knowledge of
God, and we take captive every thought
to make it obedient to Christ.*
2 Corinthians 10:5 niv

At the start of each day, you likely spend some
time looking in the mirror as you get ready to
face the world. Later, you probably consider
what you'll eat for breakfast, or if you'll even
eat breakfast at all. On the way to school, you
might think about how your day will go as you
interact with friends and teachers—if that boy
you like will notice you, or if that bully will
pick on you again. Later, you might stress out

about getting your homework done or whether your grades will ever be good enough.

How did your thoughts go in those moments? Were you thinking about how you wished you looked different, weighed less, or had more friends? Did you assume the cute boy wouldn't notice you, or get fearful when you thought about the bully who's been bugging you? Did you panic that you had no chance of getting your homework done so your grades would surely fall? Did your thoughts, in those moments, set you up for a positive experience or a negative one?

Your mind is the most powerful force in your life. The thoughts you have control the direction of your choices and, ultimately, shape the way you experience life. Your thoughts drive your successes and failures equally. Confidence, security, self-esteem, hope, love, anger, resentment, and doom are all attitudes and expectations shaped primarily by your thoughts.

What if you reframed your mind-set, saw

yourself the way God sees you, and approached life with positivity and faith? That kind of thinking takes work though. According to the verse above, you have the power to come against the lies of the enemy that disagree with what God says and to turn your thinking over to Him by considering every thought that comes into your mind and measuring it against God's Word. Then, you need to cling to the truth and discard the lies. Easier said than done, right? But as hard as it might seem, controlling your thoughts must be possible or God wouldn't tell you to do it.

Set yourself up to have a great day, positively impact your friends, deal with difficult situations, and succeed in everything you need to do by winning the mind game. Speak life and truth into your heart through the message of your mind and you'll come out a winner every time.

WHAT'S UP?

* What negative thought patterns do you deal with? Write down some of your negative thoughts here. It's okay to be honest—no one's looking!

* How can you reshape your negative thinking to be positive? Reword the thoughts you wrote above, making them line up with what God says. Do you believe them?

* What affirming words can you begin to use as you think about yourself, your life, and your relationships? List 10–15 words that you can use in your thinking to remind yourself of truth. Make those words part of your daily self-talk.

PRAYER PROMPTS

. . . .

Morning: Pray that God would show you your beauty and worth through His eyes.

Something like this. . .

> *Dear God, thank You for making*
> *me like You and for telling me I'm*
> *beautiful and worth everything*
> *You have to offer—even Your Son,*
> *Jesus. Help me to see the truth about*
> *myself through Your eyes. Give me*
> *the words to change my thinking*
> *and the strength to believe it. Amen.*

Afternoon: Ask God to walk with you and give you grace as you interact with others. Be specific about troublesome relationships and ask Him to help you make peace.

Something like this. . .

Dear God, please help me be a bright
light of Your grace at my school today.
This can only happen if I'm in control
of my thoughts, taking the negatives
and turning them into positives. Guide
my thinking as I deal with the difficult
people in my path so that I can be an
example of Your love. Amen.

Evening: Ask Him to show you where your
thought life went off track today and to help
you wake up renewed, with healthy thinking.

Something like this. . .

Father, we both know I tried hard to
take every thought captive today, just
like You want me to. We also know
that I failed at times. Please show
me where my thinking went off
track and help me wake up with the
strength to face the truth and walk
in Your knowledge tomorrow morn-
ing. Amen.

Day 2

. . . .

BE HAPPY

. . . .

Rejoice in the Lord always. I will say it
again: Rejoice! Let your gentleness
be evident to all. The Lord is near.
PHILIPPIANS 4:4-5 NIV

Exercise, especially swimming, is usually my
happy time. I listen to worship music on a
waterproof iPod, pray, and think about the
blessings in my life. I like to use that time to
center my thoughts in a positive place. But one
day last week, it wasn't working. As I swam
my laps, I found myself worrying about the
future, regretting the past, and stressing about
the present. I felt like I'd messed everything up
and nothing was ever going to work out. Do

you ever get like that? Basically, I was having a pity party. And it was all my fault. So, I shook my head like I was clearing my thoughts and turned my focus in the opposite direction. I began to thank God for the blessings in my life—past, present, and future.

Philippians 4, quoted above, tells us to rejoice always. When I was grumbling and worrying, I was choosing to disobey God. And, yes, it was a choice. Look how easy it was to turn it around. If I couldn't control it from happening, I wouldn't have been able to stop it so easily.

The next part of that verse says we should let our attitude be seen by others. In other words, God wants us to be a good example of joyfulness in all circumstances so that people will come to know Him through us as they watch us live with joy. That's part of the reason He works in the smallest details of our lives. He wants to reach others through us.

Joy is different than happiness. Happiness

is based on people, things, and circumstances. It's fleeting. Joyfulness comes from within our hearts. It's part of who we are if we understand how God is working in our lives. As I began to practice joyfulness in the pool that day, I asked God to show me how my past pain and my present concerns could be refining me or preparing me. I let the Holy Spirit wash me with peace and confidence as He healed me from my doubt. I experienced joy simply from knowing Jesus was at work in my life.

WHAT'S UP?

* *

* What circumstances have you bogged
  down in self-pity, fear, or doubt right
  now? Write them down and ask God
  to heal the negativity.

* How can you turn negative emotions
  into joy? Practice thanking God for
  even the most difficult moments.

* What can you do to help you control your thoughts in the future?
  Look back at some of your hardest
  times. Write down the lessons God
  was teaching you or the reasons He
  allowed those things so you can apply
  that understanding when you face
  hard times in the future.

PRAYER PROMPTS

....

Morning: Pray that God would show you what you have to be thankful for today.

Something like this...

> *Dear God, thank You for all You've done in my life. I know You are constantly at work on my behalf. Please help me see Your hand in my life today. Amen.*

Afternoon: Ask God to reveal any negative emotions you've struggled with today.

Something like this...

> *Dear God, I know I've grumbled and complained today. Would You please show me where my heart strayed from Your purposes and operated outside of Your joy? Please help*

me get back on track with joyfulness
and thankfulness. Amen.

Evening: Spend some time thanking Him. Something like this. . .

Father, every good and perfect gift
in my life comes from You. Every
circumstance that causes me to worry,
every pain of loss that makes me cry,
every regret I have. . . You hold them
all in the palm of Your hand. Thank
You for walking with me through
every hard time and teaching me to
be joyful no matter what. Amen.

Day 3

**THINK BEFORE
YOU SPEAK**

*Likewise, the tongue is a small part of the body,
but it makes great boasts. Consider what a
great forest is set on fire by a small spark.*
JAMES 3:5 NIV

Have you ever been the victim of gossip? It's painful to know that people are talking negatively about you and spreading rumors, trying to hurt you. Friendships, groups, even marriages have been divided over gossip. And God hates gossip. Even so, it can be tempting—yes, even for a Christian—to get pulled into a gossip session. Sometimes it's because you might want to be cool in front of your friends. Other times it might be because you're afraid if you don't, they'll start talking about you. And, let's face it, it feels good to have information that others might not, and sharing it just might elevate you socially, even if only for a minute.

As Christians, though, we are always supposed to be working for God's purposes, pointing others toward Him. Gossiping about someone or to someone will never point them to Christ since it's not in His character to use malicious words against people.

Next time you're tempted to share some juicy details about someone, ask yourself these questions:

* Is what I'm about to share truthful?
* What are my motives for sharing it?
* What benefit is there for others if I share it?
* Does Jesus want me to hold my tongue?

Words are so powerful. One little story or accusation, whether true or not, is like a spark that can start a forest fire. God wants us to control our tongues so that we are never the cause of a forest fire in someone else's life. There is always something positive to share in place of the negative. Begin to look for the good in others and spread that around for a change.

WHAT'S UP?

* Do you struggle with gossip? Write down some instances when you have fallen into that temptation lately.

* Are there certain friends or groups of friends that tend to gossip more? Write down some ideas of how you can turn a gossip session around for good.

* Is there anyone you've wronged by spreading gossip? Write an apology to that person, then go and apologize in person.

PRAYER PROMPTS

• •

Morning: Pray that God would seal your lips from gossip today.

Something like this. . .

> *Dear God, I'm sorry that I've fallen into the temptation of gossip in the past. Help me hold my tongue today. Let nothing negative slip from my lips when I speak of others. Show me the good in others so I may share that today. Amen.*

Afternoon: Ask God to help you be an example to others as you interact.

Something like this. . .

> *Dear God, please help me stand firm in my resolve not to gossip. In doing that, give me the words I need to*

show my friends why I'm not joining
in without making them feel con-
demned by me. Help them see You.
Amen.

Evening: Ask Him to show you where you succeeded and where you failed today.
Something like this. . .

> *Father, I tried to focus on not gos-*
> *siping today. Please show me where*
> *I was successful in doing that. Also,*
> *please show me the times when I*
> *could have done better so I can learn.*
> *Amen.*

Day 4

PROTECT YOURSELF

*And now, dear brothers and sisters, one final
thing. Fix your thoughts on what is true,
and honorable, and right, and pure, and lovely,
and admirable. Think about things that
are excellent and worthy of praise.*
PHILIPPIANS 4:8 NLT

We live in a world where kids are exposed to sex
and adult situations at very young ages on TV
shows, the internet, and even on smartphones.
Chances are, you've stumbled onto examples
of that whether or not you went looking for it.
It's *almost* impossible to stay pure when faced
with all the temptations and opportunities.
But it's not impossible.

This is the time to make a plan, put in safe-guards, and stick to your commitment. One of the first ways you can guard yourself is by limiting what you see online and on TV. Yes, it's easy to access all sorts of things, but that doesn't mean you should.

Another way to help you win the battle against sexual temptation is to find a mentor (a youth leader, an aunt, an older friend who has been there) who will help you make good decisions and keep you accountable to your commitment to purity.

And most importantly, when you consider dating someone, have a conversation about where they stand on purity. If someone doesn't share your values and goals, they aren't going to be able to support you in them long-term. So ask direct questions and stand your ground. If things go well and you begin a relationship, be prepared to put on the brakes if things get heated. Just walk away.

Ultimately, your body is yours and yours

alone. You get to decide what happens to it. You will never regret holding on to your purity, but with almost complete assurance, I can guarantee you will regret letting go of it before it's right. Follow God's plan for your future, which includes your body, and you'll never be sorry.

WHAT'S UP?
....

* It's time to be real. Have you had escalating exposure to sexuality? How is it affecting you?

* What type of physical relationship are you comfortable and/or uncomfortable with? How do you think that description lines up with what God has planned for you?

* From this day forward, what is your plan when it comes to purity? Even if you've stumbled already, you can make a renewed commitment today.

PRAYER PROMPTS

• •

Morning: Pray for forgiveness if it's needed. Something like this. . .

> *Dear God, I'm sorry I haven't always shielded my eyes or avoided things I knew were wrong. Please forgive me and restore my innocence to how it was before I was exposed to things I shouldn't have seen or done. Amen.*

Afternoon: Ask God to strengthen you for the choices ahead.

Something like this. . .

> *Dear God, please help me be strong in the face of sexual temptation. Give me the resolve and words I need to get out of inappropriate*

*situations. Help me to see and
think clearly in those moments so
I don't get swept away into bad
choices. Amen.*

Evening: Thank Him for who you are.
Something like this. . .

*Father, thank You for caring so
much about me and my body that
You made me in Your image. Help
me to respect myself so that others
will. Amen.*

Day 5

FAILURE IS
AN OPTION

Meanwhile, the moment we get tired in the waiting, God's Spirit is right alongside helping us along. If we don't know how or what to pray, it doesn't matter. He does our praying in and for us, making prayer out of our wordless sighs, our aching groans. He knows us far better than we know ourselves, knows our pregnant condition, and keeps us present before God. That's why we can be so sure that every detail in our lives of love for God is worked into something good.
ROMANS 8:26-28 MSG

Have you succeeded at everything you've tried? Never failed a test? Got the lead in every play? Won every game?

Of course not. Success is great, but failure is usually more familiar to us and it's definitely where we experience the most growth. Think about it. When you win a game, do you dissect your moves and try to find new ways to do it better? You might think back over what you did, but only with the intention of replicating it the next time you play. In other words, you want to stay the same because it meant success. But the next time you play, when those same moves don't result in a victory, you might stop and reconsider your strategy and try something new the next time. You learn from your mistakes in order to have a different outcome.

For many years I allowed my failures to define me and overshadow my successes. I thought people were keeping track of how many times I messed up. I spent so much time worrying about what others thought of my weaknesses that I became consumed with trying to hide them or do so many great things that they were overshadowed.

Why is failure so feared when it really is such a tool for growth? It is never fun to fail, but learning and growing is sure fun. And failure is the stepping-stone for trying again. Let God use your weaknesses to point others to Him.

WHAT'S UP?
....

* What failures from your past drive
  you into thoughts of fear and regret?
  Write them down.

* How can you turn your fear of failure
  around to where you embrace it or at
  least allow it?

* Write down three examples of times
  when you painfully failed at something but discovered later that it was
  for your best interests that you did.

PRAYER PROMPTS

• •

Morning: Pray that God would set you up to find the success in your failure today.

Something like this. . .

> *Dear God, I know I can't win at*
> *everything, so help me have a good*
> *attitude when I fail today. Show*
> *me how You're at work even in my*
> *weaknesses. Amen.*

Afternoon: Ask God to put things in perspective.

Something like this. . .

> *Dear God, help me to enjoy each*
> *moment of this day. Whether I'm*
> *winning or losing at whatever it is*
> *I'm doing, You're on the throne of my*
> *life and I'm good with that. Amen.*

Evening: Ask God to teach you from your past.

Something like this. . .

> *Father, in these quiet moments at the*
> *end of the day, would You remind*
> *me of times in my life when I have*
> *failed at something important and*
> *thought all hope was lost, but You*
> *were at work on something big?*
> *Teach me how my failures were used*
> *for Your glory and my growth, then*
> *help me apply it in the future. Amen.*

Day 6

FIFTEEN MINUTES
OF FAME

*Jesus, knowing that they intended to come
and make him king by force, withdrew
again to a mountain by himself.*
JOHN 6:15 NIV

Our culture makes it easier than ever to be famous. All you need is a cute kid, a smart cat, or a funny accident to upload to YouTube and wait for the world to find it. Between viral videos and social media, fame is measured in numbers—numbers of followers, numbers of likes, numbers of shares. It gets exhausting to keep up with all of it and compete with others who are trying to achieve the same kind of recognition.

Consider Jesus. He had all the makings of a famous person. He had a following. He had notoriety. He had an angle—no one did miracles like He did! He could have easily basked in the glow of public glory. But what did He do? As quoted in the verse above, when He knew they were about to elevate Him, He removed Himself. On one hand, that might not make a lot of sense. Couldn't He reach more people if He let His name be spread far and wide? Maybe. But by doing that, He would have to trade His humility and peace. And He'd be pointing the world to Himself, not to His Father.

Having lots of friends or being well known isn't necessarily a bad thing. But when we exalt ourselves above our mission for the kingdom (to know Christ and to make Him known), we are missing the whole point. Seeking fame for the purpose of acceptance and popularity requires you to put your own name above all else. Instead, keep your heart humble and use your life's platform to point others to Jesus, just as He always shined His light on His Father.

WHAT'S UP?

....

* What motivation drives your inter-
  actions with others, your social media
  focus, your pursuit of popularity?

* Write a 2–3 sentence mission statement about how you want to be
  known by others. What do you want
  your lasting legacy to be?

* What are some specific ways you can
  begin to step toward that legacy?

PRAYER PROMPTS

. . . .

Morning: Pray that God would help you point others to Him today.

Something like this. . .

> *Dear God, I have good intentions,
> but sometimes it's hard to focus on
> the right things when society wants
> something else. Please help me keep
> my focus on You rather than myself
> so I can help people know You more.
> Amen.*

Afternoon: Ask God to give you an opportunity to tell someone about your faith.

Something like this. . .

> *Dear God, if my life's goal is to be a
> light for You and increase Your fame,
> then I need to be able to share my*

faith. Would You give me an oppor-
tunity to do that today? And please
help me have the right words to say.
Amen.

Evening: Ask Him to show you where you need to make adjustments in your "public" life. Something like this...

Father, sometimes I get it right and
have the right balance, but other
times I know I'm all about me.
Whether it's social media, popular-
ity at school, or notoriety at my job,
would You show me where I need
to make adjustments in my attitude
and approach? Help me set godly
goals that serve You, not me. Amen.

Day 7

MIXED MESSAGES

*"The Lord doesn't see things the way you see
them. People judge by outward appearance,
but the Lord looks at the heart."*
1 Samuel 16:7 NLT

Society screams that girls should focus on
their appearance and their sexuality. Peer
groups are often categorized by clothing
style, TV shows portray sexiness as beautiful,
and advertising is most successful if it can get
girls to believe they will be sexy if they buy in.
The world tells girls that, if they want to be
popular, successful, and find true love, sex and
sexiness are their way to go.

That message is in direct opposition to

what God says to His beautiful daughters. To YOU.

Your heavenly Father wants you to believe that you are beautifully made in His image. Your body is a treasure and is to be protected. He wants you to know that He chose you and formed you just the way He wanted you. You don't need to "sell" anything to the world because He has already declared your value.

Compare these two scenarios:

> A boy wants to spend time with you because of how sexy you dress and how attractive you are to his eyes. He has no interest in, or even knowledge of, your intellect, humor, kindness, or faith. He thinks you're sexy, so he wants you. At least for the moment.
>
> A boy notices you for your goodness, kindness, and intelligence. He is attracted to you, sure, but

first and foremost, he respects you for your strong convictions and wants to spend time with you because of the value of the relationship. He will wait forever just for a few moments of your time and the opportunity to laugh with you because you're so worth it.

Which one do you want to commit to? A reputation is hard-won, but easily lost. Decide now that you want to reject sexiness and embrace value. Ignore the mixed messages and focus on the message God has for you. You're worth it.

WHAT'S UP?

* How have you bought into the lie that sex sells? Consider your words, your wardrobe, your choices.

* What are some very specific ways you can pull yourself back on the track of modesty and self-respect?

* List some qualities that make you valuable in the sight of God and the right kind of boy.

PRAYER PROMPTS
....

Morning: Pray that God would show you how to uphold your worth in this culture.

Something like this. . .

> *Dear God, it's so hard to be modest and ignore the sexual noise in this society. Please help me to remember, today and always, that I'm Your daughter. Help me to really understand who I am, what You say about me, and how You want me to present myself. Amen.*

Afternoon: Ask God to give you strength to stand strong.

Something like this. . .

> *Dear God, worldly temptations are all around me and it would be so*

easy to slip into them. Please help me
stand strong in my convictions to
protect myself and my body from the
pressures surrounding me. Amen.

Evening: Ask Him to give you patience.
Something like this. . .

Father, as I embrace modesty and
demand respect for myself and my
body, help me to patiently wait and
not rush into dating boys who don't
value my convictions. Help me to
enjoy being on my own while You
teach me more about who You say I
am. Amen.

Day 8

....

DIAGNOSIS: NOMOPHOBIA

....

I am saying this for your benefit, not to place restrictions on you. I want you to do whatever will help you serve the Lord best, with as few distractions as possible.
1 CORINTHIANS 7:35 NLT

Where's your phone? Chances are you didn't even blink when I asked that. It's most likely right beside you, if not in your hand. Nomophobia is the fear of being out of the reach of phone contact—lost phone, dead battery, no network coverage available. It is a name for the anxiety that is caused by not having access to your phone. Do you have that sickness? I'm going to be honest with you, and this might come as a surprise. I definitely have nomophobia, and I didn't even realize it!

Signs you've got nomophobia:

* You sleep with your phone right beside you.

* You take your phone to the bathroom.

* You check your social media and/or texts excessively, obsessively, and absentmindedly.

* You feel stress if you're in one room and your phone is in another.

Phones aren't bad, but reliance on them to that degree definitely is. God wants us to focus on Him first—to let Him be our first line of contact and our first thought when we want connection with others. As stated in the verse above, He isn't trying to keep us from something good. He simply wants us to serve Him and to avoid distractions that will get between us and Him. He's clear about that because He knows how easily our eyes are diverted from our purpose, and He wants the best for us, which is relationship with Him.

WHAT'S UP?

. . . .

* Do you have nomophobia? Describe your attachment to your mobile devices.

* Describe what would happen if you left your phone home and turned off today. How would you feel?

* How can you take steps to loosen your grip on your phone and turn your eyes more toward Jesus?

PRAYER PROMPTS

....

Morning: Pray that God would help you loosen your grip on technology.

Something like this. . .

> *Dear God, thank You for the gift*
> *of technology, including my phone.*
> *Please help me keep it in the right*
> *perspective and to release the hold*
> *it has on my life. Remove the*
> *distraction that comes between us.*
> *Amen.*

Afternoon: Ask God to show you ways you have relied too heavily on your mobile devices today.

Something like this. . .

> *Dear God, I'm trying, but this culture*
> *is so driven by phones that it's hard*

to change. How have I allowed my
phone to affect my purpose today?
Please help me fix it right now.
Amen.

Evening: Ask Him to empower you to do even better tomorrow.

Something like this. . .

Father, today was better, but I know
I've got a long way to go. Please
continue to work on me, showing
me how I need to focus on You with
nothing between us. Amen.

Day 9

WHEN GOD GETS IT WRONG

And this is the confidence that we have toward him, that if we ask anything according to his will he hears us.
1 JOHN 5:14 ESV

I recently faced a huge crossroads in my life. Huge. I prayed that God would open one specific door and close another. I was SURE, beyond a shadow of a doubt, that the direction I thought I needed to go was the right one. And I was sure God agreed because, well, it made perfect sense, and He's pretty smart. . .so. . .

Yeah, I'm sure you know where this is

headed. Not only did He open neither door, but He kept me right where I was. I didn't get it. I quoted Him to Him: You said You'd give if I ask! You said You heard my prayers! You said that all I had to do was present my requests! What's up?

When Jesus first started to perform miracles, no one knew what He was capable of so they had no real expectations. Then, as time went on and His power became evident through the miracles He performed, expectations like mine increased. It's easy to assume that just because He CAN do something, He WILL do it. But is that really what we want? Do we want to pull up to God's drive-thru window and order up our lives like we would a burger and fries?

As nice as that might sound, do you realize the limitations that presents? If you're the one calling the shots, that means you're limited to your own vision and understanding. You become your own "god." However, when you've surrendered to God's will and plan for your life, it might not always make sense, and it might even seem like He gets it wrong at times, but in the end, all will be revealed and you'll be so glad you didn't end up with things the way you thought you wanted them.

WHAT'S UP?

* *

* Looking back, when have you seen God say no or not yet? How did you respond?

* What have you been striving for that has made you question God's wisdom?

* Write a statement where you surrender your will and embrace God's will for your life.

PRAYER PROMPTS

Morning: Pray with thanksgiving over the blessings in your life.

Something like this...

> *Dear God, I want to start this day*
> *not asking for anything, but rather*
> *with a reminder of how awesome*
> *You are. Thank You for the amazing*
> *blessings in my life. Help me to cher-*
> *ish them today. Amen.*

Afternoon: Ask God for help trading your wants for His way.

Something like this...

> *Dear God, You know I've been ask-*
> *ing You _____ lately. Although*
> *I want that thing in the worst*
> *way, I'm willing to surrender my*

will and desires to Your perfect plan. Help me to release my expectations. Amen.

Evening: Ask Him to give you peace about His plan.

Something like this...

Father, thank You for having a plan for me even if I can't always see or understand it. Help me to trust You no matter what, and to accept it when You tell me no or not yet with as much joy as I do when You tell me yes. Amen.

Day 10

ONLINE VS.
OFFLINE

· ·

Finally, brothers and sisters,
whatever is true, whatever is noble,
whatever is right, whatever is pure,
whatever is lovely, whatever is
admirable—if anything is excellent
or praiseworthy—think about
such things.
PHILIPPIANS 4:8 NIV

True character is defined by what you do when no one is looking. So your words and actions, even in a pseudo-anonymous online setting, are as important to defining your true self as are the things you say and do offline. If you are negative, hurtful, crass, inappropriate, gossipy, or rude on social media, then that means you are those things in your heart.

You can't type something you haven't first thought. And you can't insult someone if you haven't first searched for their supposed flaws. You can't share something inappropriate unless you first let it past your own filter. You can't gossip online if you haven't let those intentions enter your will and become your actions.

Online is not a safe house for a secret you. It's you on display for the whole world to see. How do you want to be defined?

The Bible says we're to think and share things that uplift others, that are admirable and praiseworthy. We're to filter our thoughts and experiences through a lens of purity, love, honesty, and righteousness. Have you ever tried to apply those principles to your online activity?

WHAT'S UP?

* Consider your recent activity online and on social media. What things have you participated in that are outside of God's filters?

* How can you reshape your presence on social media into something that reflects the verse quoted above?

* Think of two times you've said something you shouldn't have online. How could you have said it better?

PRAYER PROMPTS

....

Morning: Pray that God would open your eyes to your behavior.

Something like this. . .

> *Dear God, please be present with me today. Help me to know right away if I'm using technology as a veil to hide bad behavior. Let me be an example of You in person, online, and when using social media. Amen.*

Afternoon: Ask God to help you make a real difference.

Something like this. . .

> *Dear God, I encounter situations all the time where I see bullying, gossip, or other inappropriate behavior*

online. Please help me know when to step in and exactly how I should handle it. Let me always have the right motives. Amen.

Evening: Thank Him for guarding your words. Something like this. . .

Father, thank You for making me aware of my double standards. Please help me to continue to do better and better so that I'm a constant example of You, even on Snapchat. Amen.

Day 11

BE YOU-NIQUE

Dear friends, you are like foreigners and strangers in this world. I beg you to avoid the evil things your bodies want to do that fight against your soul. People who do not believe are living all around you and might say that you are doing wrong. Live such good lives that they will see the good things you do and will give glory to God on the day when Christ comes again.
1 PETER 2:11–12 NCV

How important is it to you that you're different from your classmates? Maybe you go for uniqueness by having a different hairstyle or setting your own clothing trends. Or maybe you, like many, get so caught up in the desire to please the people around you that you end up with the same outward style and the same tastes in music, movies, and television. It's safe and natural to want to conform to the world around you, but it's not how God wants His followers to live.

In 1 Peter 2:11 (above), He tells us that we are to live among the people of this world as if we are guests. Our time here is temporary and it's all for His purposes. He warns us not to get caught up in pleasing people, get sucked into sinful behaviors, or get so focused on fitting in that we aren't an example of Christ. Verse 12 goes on to explain why this is so important: ". . .that they will see the good things you do and will give glory to God."

How should you be YOU-nique?

* Let the Holy Spirit convict you of sin.

* Live in such a way that others will know you've got something they want.

* Let your words and actions bring glory to God.

WHAT'S UP?

∗ What are some sinful ways that you
   are conforming to the patterns of the
   world? Be honest.

∗ How can you turn those behaviors
   around for good?

∗ What are some ways that you can
   intentionally be different for Jesus?

PRAYER PROMPTS

· ·

Morning: Pray that God would give you the strength to stand out.

Something like this. . .

> *Dear God, I want to be crazy differ-*
> *ent for You. I want my life to stand*
> *out among my peers as an example of*
> *who You are in my life. I want there*
> *to be no mistake today and every day*
> *that I'm a Christ follower. Please*
> *help me overcome my tendency to*
> *blend in. Amen.*

Afternoon: Ask God to give you a new opportunity to be different.

Something like this. . .

> *Dear God, okay, I've fixed some*
> *areas where I was headed down the*

wrong path. Now would You show
me how I can be radically different?
Use me today like never before so I
can see You working through me in
the lives of others around me. Amen.

Evening: Ask Him to show you where your thoughts went astray today and to help you wake up refreshed, with Christlike thinking.

Something like this. . .

Father, I'm beginning to see how so
much of my life has been to please
others. Going forward, please help
me identify each moment when that's
the case and turn it around for Your
glory. Amen.

Day 12

IT'S A DATE

· ·

Therefore, if anyone is in Christ,
the new creation has come:
The old has gone, the new is here!
2 CORINTHIANS 5:17 NIV

My parents had a rule that I couldn't date until I turned sixteen. But when I was fifteen, a youth leader from my church started showing an interest in me. My parents liked and trusted him, so they let me start dating him six months before my sixteenth birthday.

He was amazing. Older. Mature. Godly. He made me feel special and important and valuable. We spent a lot of time together in the two and a half years we dated. And the best part was that he never pressured me in any way. He said he would respect the boundaries that we had both set, and he did. I never felt at risk or concerned that things would escalate beyond what we could handle.

That sounds great, doesn't it? But even though it turned out great, I got a bit older and, as I matured into more of an adult, I realized that the fifteen-year-old me was long gone and I needed to let go of the things of the past. That even though things had gone well, he wasn't the man I was to marry. We had a very painful breakup, and it left scars.

Your experiences will be different than mine. But I can assure you that we will share one component for sure. The fifteen-year-old you is a very different person than the twenty-five-year-old you will be. Don't make choices (date the wrong guy, go too far physically, etc.) at fifteen or sixteen that you'll still regret when you're older. I'm so glad that I didn't let the excitement of a long-term dating relationship cause me to weaken my resolve or change my boundaries. In the end, I had nothing to regret.

Surrender this area of your life to God and allow Him to guide your steps. You see, He already knows the woman you'll be and wants to save you from the pain of early mistakes. Let Him walk you through these years with His eyes on the future He has planned for you. Jesus promises to fill you with His love, so much so that you don't even need to look for love in the dating world. Find it in Him first.

WHAT'S UP?

* *

* Do you feel the need to date right now? Why?

* What scares you about not dating during your teen years?

* If you choose to date, what are some boundaries you intend to keep?

PRAYER PROMPTS
....

Morning: Pray that God will fill you with His love.

Something like this. . .

> *Dear God, I know in my head that
> it's okay if I don't have a boyfriend,
> but someone needs to tell it to my
> heart. Will You fill me with Your
> love and presence so I have no need
> to feel love from others? Help me
> walk with You so I never feel alone.
> Amen.*

Afternoon: Ask Him for a godly distraction.

Something like this. . .

> *Dear God, I want to spend my teen
> years learning and growing into the
> woman You want me to be. Please*

help me take steps toward that person. Show me where to go so I can dive deeper into You during this time. Amen.

Evening: Pray for protection. Something like this. . .

Father, as I meet people and explore the idea of dating, please protect my heart, mind, and body from the things of the world. I want to make the right choices and not get swept up in emotion. Please keep me focused on what's right. Amen.

Day 13

CHANGE IS GOOD

For to set the mind on the flesh is death,
but to set the mind on the Spirit
is life and peace.
ROMANS 8:6 ESV

New school. Off to college. Relocation. Those are big ones. Change can come in smaller packages too. New kid at school. Auditions for a new play. New procedures at work. Life is full of big and small changes. We expect it and plan for it. Some of us even like it!

So if we know change is inevitable, why do we act surprised when it comes? Why do we allow change to stop us in our tracks?

I believe that anxiety in the face of change is nothing more than a signal of a lack of faith. If you love where you're at so much that you struggle with changing your circumstances, then it means you don't trust in what God has waiting for you on the other side. It means you're more interested in what God has already done for you and leery about what He has planned next. What if it's not as good? What if it's going to hurt? What if you're not happy? All of those questions and fears are wrapped around one thing—yourself.

You might be facing a big change right now (if not, bookmark this page because it will come!) that has your brain racing at full speed. Take a deep breath and find some time to be alone with the Lord and rest. Reset your mind, walk forward boldly, and pray for peace. Bask in the glow of His presence and allow the Holy Spirit to remind you that He's got this. In a few minutes, you'll begin to feel the peace of God wash over you as you release your control and open your heart to His plan.

WHAT'S UP?

* Can you think of times you've feared
   change in your life? What was the
   outcome?

* What looming changes or fears are
   clawing at your thoughts right now?

* How can you rewrite the words of
   your fears to turn them into faith-
   filled expectations?

PRAYER PROMPTS

....

Morning: Pray that God would use change for your good today.

Something like this. . .

> *Dear God, I'm a creature of habit,*
> *so help me break my hold on the*
> *routines of my life and embrace the*
> *newness You want to unfold. Help*
> *me see where You're at work so I can*
> *have faith that each little change is*
> *for my good. Amen.*

Afternoon: Pray that God will remind you of when change was good.

Something like this. . .

> *Dear God, please help me remember*
> *times when I faced scary changes and*
> *how You came through for me. Show*

me that Your hand was at work
at all times. Thank You for walk-
ing with me through every tough
moment. Amen.

Evening: Ask God to excite you about change.
Something like this. . .

Father, now that I get the reason
that change is good, help me to look
for and embrace it with all my heart,
not fight it and barely suffer through
it. Let me see it as an opportunity to
step closer into who You are prepar-
ing me to be. Amen.

Day 14

THEY DON'T
UNDERSTAND ME!

*"Honor your father and mother" is the first
commandment that has a promise attached
to it, namely, "so you will live
well and have a long life."*
EPHESIANS 6:2-3 MSG

There's not a teenager alive, ever, who didn't
feel misunderstood by her parents. Sometimes
that's simply due to changing times and cul-
tures that create a gulf in communication and
expectations. Other times, it's because the
parents don't really see what is going on in
the heart and mind of their teen so they can't

speak to the real issues. Both of those obstacles stem from a problem with communication.

Communication, though, is more than just words. It's honest expression that conveys the full depth of the reality of a situation. If you keep your conversation on the surface, about television, clothes, movies, chores, school, etc., then you're only offering a glimpse of the real you. If you don't share your fears, longings, regrets, joys, sorrows, and pains with your parents, how can they effectively communicate with you? (Trust me, I would say the same thing to them too.) For example, if they ask you how your day was and you answer with the same monotone "fine" you say every day, how are they to know that someone hurt your feelings or you're being bullied? How can they help you with your fears of getting into the right college if you don't talk about the choice you have to make?

The connection you have with your parents will be one of the longest-lasting relationships you will have in your life. Think about it. Friends will come and go. Even a spouse doesn't arrive on the scene until your parents have been around for a couple of decades. Protect this vital relationship even now by establishing good communication—the key to making it a loving and fulfilling experience for all of you.

WHAT'S UP?

....

* What negativity do you recite in your
  brain about your parents? Get it out
  here, once and for all.

* How can you reshape those negative
  thoughts into more loving thoughts?
  Try it now.

* What things do you need to communicate with your parents about?
  Try writing out some statements you
  could share with them later.

PRAYER PROMPTS

....

Morning: Pray that God would guard your lips today.

Something like this. . .

> *Dear God, thank You for my parents. I don't know what I'd do without them. Please help me choose kind words toward them today, keeping my bad attitude in check. Amen.*

Afternoon: Ask God to give you an open heart to dialogue honestly with your parents.

Something like this. . .

> *Dear God, I've held a lot back from my parents because I've been judging them. Please help me open my heart to share with them more so I can*

allow them to embrace the real me.
Help me to receive their efforts, even
if they fumble a bit. Amen.

Evening: Pray for your parents.
Something like this. . .

> *Father, it's becoming clear to me that*
> *my parents truly do love me. You've*
> *tasked them with quite a job and*
> *they're doing their best. Help them to*
> *keep up the good work and to have*
> *peace about our family. Please help*
> *them see that I want to be different*
> *and partner with them on this jour-*
> *ney of family. Amen.*

Day 15

·······························

IT'S NOT OKAY

·······························

Do not take revenge, my dear friends,
but leave room for God's wrath, for it is written:
"It is mine to avenge; I will repay," says the Lord.
ROMANS 12:19 NIV

Sometimes forgiveness comes easily because we can tell the person recognized the hurt they caused and is genuinely sorry. But sometimes a wrong is committed that seems beyond the reach of forgiveness. Abuse. Rejection. Abandonment. Slander. How is it possible for a human being to offer forgiveness for those things, especially when the person isn't sorry and you're still hurting?

Did you know that Jesus died for you

before you acknowledged your sin? The forgiveness was done and available to you before you ever reached for it. And Jesus cried out to His Father to forgive His accusers even while He hung on the cross.

No, we aren't Jesus. That's true. We don't have godlike power and compassion. Or do we? Actually, we do. We have, within us, the full measure of the love and forgiveness of Christ. In fact, as quoted in the verse above, He carried the burden to right our wrongs. We need only forgive and love, leaving the rest up to Him. Sin is not ignored—not theirs and not yours. It's paid for. The blood that covered your sins also covered theirs.

However, forgiveness doesn't erase the pain and it doesn't necessarily restore the relationships. It only says, "You know what, I'm not going to hold you accountable or seek revenge for what you've done. I'm going to love you with the love of Christ." And then it lets go. In time, pain dulls and sometimes relationships are restored, but those things aren't the goal and they aren't promised.

You can't offer true forgiveness on your own, but with His help, you can!

WHAT'S UP?

* *

✲ What wrongs have you committed for which others have forgiven you?

✲ Who are you struggling to forgive?

✲ What makes it difficult to offer forgiveness? Really search your heart on this one.

PRAYER PROMPTS

●●●●●●●●●●●●●●●●●●●●●●●●●●●●

Morning: Pray that God would show you the depths of His forgiveness for you.

Something like this. . .

> *Dear God, thank You for forgiving me of my sins. Please give me a glimpse of that to help me understand the full scope of what it means so I can really know the price You paid for me. Amen.*

Afternoon: Ask Him to reveal bitterness and unforgiveness in your heart.

Something like this. . .

> *Dear God, I know I'm holding on to some things, and sometimes they just eat me up inside. Would You help me identify the root of my anger and*

bitterness so I can begin the process of
dealing with it? Amen.

Evening: Ask Him to give you the strength
to truly forgive those who have wronged you.
Something like this. . .

> *Father, I feel pain in places You*
> *already know about. I want to be*
> *free of bitterness, free to love, and*
> *free to forgive. I can't do it in my*
> *own strength. Please help me. Amen.*

Day 16

····························

RANDOM ACTS

····························

Get rid of all bitterness, rage, anger, harsh
words, and slander, as well as all types
of evil behavior. Instead, be kind to each
other, tenderhearted, forgiving one
another, just as God through
Christ has forgiven you.
EPHESIANS 4:31–32 NLT

I know a woman who paid for the purchases
of the woman behind her at McDonald's one
evening. A few minutes later, as my friend was
parked to the side, doling out food to her kids,
there was a knock at her window. It was the
woman whose meal my friend paid for. She
said, "I want you to know that I was buying

dinner for my three kids. I was going to give it to them, and then go upstairs and take enough pills to kill myself. Your small act of kindness reminded me that I'm not alone. It doesn't matter that my husband left us or that I lost my job. I'm not alone."

Wow. What a lesson. What if my friend hadn't listened to the prompting of the Holy Spirit in that moment? Would that troubled mom actually have taken her life? Ultimately though, she drove away from there reminded that she had value and a real place in the world. It cost my friend about twenty bucks, but it gave those kids a renewed mom and gave that woman peace and worth. As Christians, even young ones, we need to be on high alert, open to the gentle nudging of God to offer kindness to a lost and dying world.

Do you lash out at your siblings when they get on your nerves? Do you stomp off in a huff when your parents discipline you? Do you spread gossip about someone at school who has wronged you? Let's turn all of those things on their head and, instead of repaying bad for bad, try showing kindness when you're upset. Doing something kind for someone you're mad at will help you overcome that selfish, bad attitude every single time. Try it!

WHAT'S UP?

* Ask yourself some important questions. Do you really want to be kind? Why or why not? Are you only kind when you want something in return? Is that okay?

* Make a short list of things that people have recently done to make you mad.

* For each item in the list above, write an example of a kindness you could show that person.

PRAYER PROMPTS

....

Morning: Pray that God would help you hold your temper today.

    Something like this. . .

> *Dear God, I know people are going to annoy me or even make me mad today. Please help me keep a lid on my temper and choose my responses wisely so I don't do or say something I'll regret. Amen.*

Afternoon: Ask Him to give you an opportunity to show extreme kindness to an unlikely person.

    Something like this. . .

> *Dear God, I love the idea of being kind to people who aren't necessarily on my happy list. I love it because it's*

*Your heart, so I want it to be mine
too. Please give me an opportunity to
do that today—show me what You've
prepared for me and then give me the
courage to carry it out. Amen.*

Evening: Ask Him to teach you from your experiences.

Something like this. . .

*Father, I think I'm getting it. Would
You show me the effect my kindness
had on others today? What could I
have done differently? Please help me
stay focused on being kind, not right.
Amen.*

Day 17

FITTING IN

"You are the light of the world. A city set on a hill cannot be hidden. Nor do people light a lamp and put it under a basket, but on a stand, and it gives light to all in the house. In the same way, let your light shine before others, so that they may see your good works and give glory to your Father who is in heaven."
MATTHEW 5:14–16 ESV

There is something about the passage above that really inspires me to go out and make a difference. Just think about it. As Christ followers, we are on display to the world. This isn't meant to be a burden to our lifestyles, but as a privilege to our calling. We are the light that illuminates Christ to a dark and dying world. Wow. That's pretty awesome! But with that amazing privilege comes huge responsibility. It means that we need to actually portray Christ in our lives so that when people turn our way, they see something different, something they want.

It's great to fit in and be accepted by our peers, but it can be difficult to be that bright light we are called to be when we're with a group of people who share different values. But it's not impossible—it just requires intentional effort and the willingness to be different. It's vital that, wherever you go and even among your peers at school, your words and actions reflect the light of Christ so they can know Him through you.

Be okay with not quite fitting in. Be okay with floating on the fringe of the groups you're a part of. It's only because your friends can see there's something different about you, even if they can't quite pinpoint what it is. So set your boundaries and make them clear, say no when you need to, and build godly friendships to help strengthen you.

This world is temporary and our relationships are temporary. Don't let the reactions of others become more important than God's purpose for you.

WHAT'S UP?

* *

* Why do you want to fit in?

* Describe some times when you have made mistakes because of your desire to fit in.

* What are three tips you can pull right from today's reading that will help you be a light to your friends?

PRAYER PROMPTS
• •

Morning: Pray that God would use you as a bright light today.

Something like this. . .

> *Dear God, I give You my heart, my words, and my actions—I give You my day—to use as You wish. Give me the courage to stand and shine brightly wherever I am. Amen.*

Afternoon: Ask Him to forgive you for times when your light has been dim.

Something like this. . .

> *Dear God, now that my resolve is burning brightly, I can see times when I've not carried the torch. Please forgive me for putting my desire to fit in above You. May I*

always shine brightly for You! Amen.

Evening: Ask Him to renew your thinking about popularity and fitting in.

Something like this. . .

> *Father, I want to live and move within a kingdom perspective—so that everything I do is for You. I want to care more about shining and telling others about You than I do about being popular. Please help me to remember that every day. Amen.*

Day 18

....

WIN THE RACE

....

Do you not know that in a race all the runners run, but only one receives the prize? So run that you may obtain it. Every athlete exercises self-control in all things. They do it to receive a perishable wreath, but we an imperishable.
1 CORINTHIANS 9:24-25 ESV

Why does the Bible talk about being a servant and that the last will be first in the kingdom, but then, as mentioned above, instruct us to try to win? That doesn't even make sense.

Here's the deal with that. I do triathlons and some running races. I train all year long in swimming, biking, and running. Last year I was so happy and proud to complete a Half

Ironman (a 1.2-mile swim, a 56-mile bike ride, and a half marathon). People asked me if I hoped to win. I laughed. I knew that if all went well, I'd finish with the masses, somewhere in the middle. But I would finish! Then they would ask me why I was training so hard if I didn't think I'd win.

Good question.

To me, the bigger point in the race was the journey. I trained like a champion because I believed in the journey to the finish line. I gave it my all every step of the way and I cried at the end. I cried with joy because I finished well, and I cried with sadness because it was over. The journey—putting one sore foot in front of the other, swimming at 5 a.m. on very cold days, biking during heat waves with a sore leg—proved to me what I was made of.

Those moments are what I take with me.

We each have a spiritual race set before us, and God has a training plan for our journey, which He outlines in His Word. Sometimes the Christian life is difficult—much like training for a triathlon. We strive and then grow weak. But when we do grow weak, that's when we turn to Him for strength. You've got this, sister.

WHAT'S UP?

* *

* How are you feeling on your spiritual
   journey right now?

* How does my Ironman analogy trans-
   late to your journey with Christ? How
   are you training your spirit?

* What are some ways you can improve
   your training as you continue the race
   set before you?

PRAYER PROMPTS

. . . .

Morning: Pray that God would strengthen you for today's training.

Something like this. . .

> *Dear God, I'm showing up at the*
> *starting line. Please give me the tools*
> *to do the work I need to finish today's*
> *leg of the race, and help me train*
> *well along the way. Amen.*

Afternoon: Ask God to rejuvenate you for the next steps.

Something like this. . .

> *Dear God, sometimes, like right*
> *now, I feel weary and just want to*
> *give up. It's hard to stay focused on*
> *the work when the results (the finish*
> *line) seem so far away. Please renew*

my spirit and give me energy for my
next steps. Amen.

Evening: Ask Him to show you where your training can be improved.

Something like this. . .

Father, I'm open to what You have
for me or want from me. Please show
me the direction You would have
me go and I will do it with a happy
heart. Amen.

Day 19

WHO AM I?

No, in all these things we are more than conquerors through him who loved us.
ROMANS 8:37 NIV

Teens of all shapes, sizes, and colors deal with eating disorders. You might be battling that stronghold right now, or you likely know someone who is.

There are different kinds of eating disorders, but they usually stem from the same thing. They are rarely about food and almost always about self-acceptance, control, and fear. If a teenager can accept herself, negative words of others have little effect. Conversely, if someone doesn't accept herself, even the kindest words fall on deaf ears. And when life spins out of control, if you can control what you eat, the pain may dull. The last component is fear—fear of not being liked, fear of gaining weight, fear of. . . You get the idea.

If you think you might have an eating disorder, it's up to you to take the first step. You first need to decide that you want to change the destructive path you're on. Then you need to own your eating behaviors so you can address them. Finally, you need to be honest about the feelings you have that led you to this place.

The best part is that you are not alone. God loves you so much that He made you like Him. You are a reflection of Him. And He loves you so extravagantly that He sent His Son to die for you. He is with you every step of the way. But you also need supportive people you can trust who will help you take this seriously and get you the help you need.

Start with your parents, a youth pastor, or a trusted teacher.

You are not alone on this journey. Today is the day to take the first step.

WHAT'S UP?

. . . .

✳ What thoughts or fears are driving
  you to disordered eating behaviors?

✳ How can you reshape your negative
  thinking into positive? Talk to yourself like Jesus would respond to what
  you wrote above.

✳ What affirming words can you begin
  to use as you think about yourself?
  List 10–15 words that you can use in
  your thinking to remind yourself of
  truth. Make those words part of your
  daily self-talk.

PRAYER PROMPTS

• •

Morning: Pray that God would help you see yourself through His eyes today.

Something like this. . .

> *Dear God, I'm struggling to see my worth, let alone my beauty. In my darkness, I'm making destructive choices about my body. Please help me see clearly and make healthier choices one day at a time. Amen.*

Afternoon: Ask God to fill you with His acceptance.

Something like this. . .

> *Dear God, sometimes I get so lonely in this body of mine. I don't even feel like anyone can see me. Will You just flood me with Your love and*

acceptance so I know You're there?
Amen.

Evening: Ask Him to show you what you did right today.

Something like this. . .

> *Father, thank You for helping me get*
> *through the day making better eating*
> *choices than yesterday. Help me to*
> *remember to lean on You every day*
> *like I did today. Amen.*

Day 20

. . . .

THE TITHE

. . . .

"Bring the whole tithe into the storehouse,
that there may be food in my house. Test me in
this," says the LORD Almighty, "and see if I will
not throw open the floodgates of heaven
and pour out so much blessing that there
will not be room enough to store it."
MALACHI 3:10 NIV

I know you may not have a ton of cash sitting
around, but it is good to establish moral practices now, rather than waiting until bad habits
are already in place. Tithing is basically giving 10 percent of your income to the church.
The Israelites, as shown above, were required
to pay a tithe to the temple. Although many

Christians tithe as a principle of giving to God first before spending on other things, there is nothing in the New Testament that suggests tithing is still a rule.

There's probably a little voice in your ear saying, "This is great. You can keep your money! Or, if you want to give something, how about 5 percent or whatever feels right in the moment?" Before you get too excited that you don't have to tithe, I'm going to suggest that it should go deeper than that. Instead of shaving 10 percent off the top of your earnings, how about 100 percent?

Jesus gave all. He held nothing back. He laid down His very life for each of us in the ultimate offering of all time. I believe that He does call us to give 100 percent of everything we've got for His work. Our time, our talent, and our resources. It's all His to use as He sees fit, for His purposes.

The struggle with that mentality is that it requires you to be in tune with the Holy Spirit so you can move when He says to. How do you know how much money to give in the offering each week? He'll show you. How do you know which ministries to get involved in? He'll tell you. How do you know when it's time to be an extravagant giver of your resources? He'll make it known if you're open to Him.

It all comes down to having a heart of surrender.

WHAT'S UP?
....

✻ What tithing/offering practices have
  been modeled for you at home? If you
  don't know where your parents stand
  on this issue, you should ask them.

✻ What do you believe about the surrender of your stuff to God?

✻ What financial/spiritual practices can
  you begin to employ now that you can
  take into the rest of your life?

PRAYER PROMPTS

••••••••••••••••••••••••••••

Morning: Pray that God would help you control your spending today.

Something like this. . .

> *Dear God, thank You for all the gifts*
> *You've given me. Please help me use*
> *my money wisely, not wastefully,*
> *and to do something good with*
> *everything You've entrusted to me.*
> *Amen.*

Afternoon: Ask for wisdom with a lifelong plan.

Something like this. . .

> *Dear God, I'm a little confused about*
> *what You want from me. I want*
> *to do the right thing. Please show*
> *me what that is so I can be a good*

steward of the things of this world.
Amen.

Evening: Ask Him to open your heart.
Something like this. . .

> *Father, I want to meet needs in Your*
> *name and live generously. Please*
> *help me to do that by showing me*
> *where I need to apply my resources.*
> *Let me see where You're at work so I*
> *can join You there. Amen.*

Day 21

FORCED FELLOWSHIP

Be on your guard and stay awake. Your enemy,
the devil, is like a roaring lion, sneaking
around to find someone to attack.
1 PETER 5:8 CEV

More and more I hear that teenagers resent that their parents make them go to church. They almost always follow that comment with something like, "Oh, I still love God. I just don't like church." When asked why, they make comments about the music, the messages, the older people, and, my favorite, Sunday is their only day to sleep in. Do you share in any of those thoughts? Or maybe you have reasons of your own. If you're one of those teens, what would you prefer that church is like? What would make you want to be there and get more involved?

First of all, church, as a building, is not the answer to Christianity. Keith Green, a singer/songwriter from the '70s, once said that going to church doesn't make you a Christian any more than going to McDonald's makes you a hamburger. But church is supposed to be set apart, not like the rest of the world that clamors for your time and attention. It's a place of rest and renewal, a place to focus on what's most important in life. It's an open place to explore your heart and get guidance for your future. It's a safe place to ask questions, dig deep, and get to know Jesus even more.

Do you feel that way at your church? If not, is the problem with you or the church. . .maybe both? Maybe your heart and mind need to be more open to what God wants you to learn and experience at your church. And maybe He has plans for how you can help institute some changes and usher the church body into the next generation of style and trends to make it more interesting to people your age.

Be aware that Satan would prefer you not go to church for all the reasons I listed above. You must close your ears to his lies and not allow his schemes to pull your eyes from such an important tool in your Christian walk.

WHAT'S UP?

* What negative thoughts have clouded your view of your church, in specific, or the broader church overall?

* What purposes does God have for a community of believers fellowshipping together at a church?

* What are some ways you could become more involved in your church?

PRAYER PROMPTS

. . . .

Morning: Pray that God would show you the value in assembling with your church body.

Something like this. . .

> *Dear God, please help me understand*
> *why it's so important to be a part*
> *of my church and to attend so often.*
> *Help me to have an open mind and*
> *pure heart when I walk in the doors*
> *so I can learn. Amen.*

Afternoon: Pray for your church body and the leaders.

Something like this. . .

> *Dear God, thank You for the Chris-*
> *tian leaders and friends You've*
> *brought into my life. I treasure them*
> *and want to learn from them. Please*

guide them as they lead, teach, and mentor me in life. Give me an open mind to soak up what they have for me. Amen.

Evening: Ask Him to show you your role. Something like this. . .

Father, I know the church is full of all kinds of different people and we all aren't called to be the same thing. Would You begin to show me what role You have for me so I can start doing my part in the church? Amen.

Day 22

I'M SORRY

Therefore, confess your sins to one another and pray for one another, that you may be healed. The prayer of a righteous person has great power as it is working.
JAMES 5:16 ESV

I'm sorry.

What is it about those two little words that makes them so difficult to say? It is because they require a deliberate act of will, the laying down of one's pride—HUMILITY above all! There is no such thing as a perfect person. Yet, when it comes to confessing to your parents that you have wronged them, you flinch, you want to duck and cover. You can internalize your error—stuff it down and keep it hidden—because it is just too hard to "fess up" and admit to your parents that you are not perfect. Humility is the peacemaker that has the ability to mend relationships. Now it's time to put it into practice.

* Let humility rule your heart, and be quick to confess.

* Seek God's help in the process of laying down that ugly face of pride when it rears its head.

* Listen to that feeling in your gut that tells you when you need to apologize. . . that's the Holy Spirit!

* Take advantage of every opportunity to confess your wrongs. In doing so, you are modeling the character of Christ and encouraging others to do likewise!

WHAT'S UP?

* How have your parents modeled humility by apologizing to each other and to you?

* How has their example affected your ability to admit when you have wronged your friends or family?

* Is there a situation for which you need to apologize to someone? Write down the words you can say.

PRAYER PROMPTS

• •

Morning: Pray that God will mold your heart into one of genuine humility. Ask God to show you new ways to be humble each day. Something like this. . .

> *Dear God, thank You for making me like You. Because I'm made in Your image, I know that I can strive for authentic humility in my life. Help me to be humble, especially when I feel tempted to prove someone else is wrong. I believe that as You help me grow in humility, I will see the positive impact is has on my relationships. Amen.*

Afternoon: Ask God to encourage a repentant attitude within you. Ask Him to gently nudge you when you're being stubborn and unapologetic.

Something like this. . .

> *Dear God, please help me to always repent when I know I'm in the wrong. Remind me that not only do I need to ask You for forgiveness; I also must ask forgiveness from those I've hurt. No one likes a friend who can never say they're sorry or admit that they're wrong. Amen.*

Evening: Pray that God will provide you with strength to overcome nasty, prideful feelings.

Something like this. . .

> *Father, none of us are immune to the ugly sin of pride. I ask that You will remove pridefulness from my heart and attitude. Remind me that pride only gets in the way of love and truth. Do not let me destroy relationships with my loved ones over foolish pride. Amen.*

Day 23

....

PLEASE PASS THE SALT

....

"You are the salt of the earth. But if the salt loses its saltiness, how can it be made salty again? It is no longer good for anything, except to be thrown out and trampled underfoot."
MATTHEW 5:13 NIV

A chef spends hours perfecting a new recipe and grabs a tasting spoon to offer a sample to a guest. What's the most likely comment a person might use if they sense something is off with the recipe? "It could use some salt." Salt is the most commonly used spice because it enhances everything it touches, and it doesn't take much to make a huge impact on the food it seasons.

I once heard that if all the salt was pulled from the ocean and spread across the earth, it would make a layer thicker than five hundred feet over the whole earth. That's a lot of salt!

Now, imagine the effects just a dash of salt has on a dish. Compare that to a five-hundred-foot layer of salt on the earth. That's the effect your Christian witness is meant to have on the world. As a Christian, you're meant to spice up the world around you by adding flavor that brings out the best of what Jesus has to offer.

Sometimes teens have a hard time being open about their faith because they're afraid that people will judge them or make fun of them. Do you ever feel that way? But those who stand boldly and confidently, sharing truth without shame or apology, are living as the salt they are called to be.

It doesn't matter how the spice is received; it only matters that Christians do their part and let God sort it out.

WHAT'S UP?

....

* Who has had a direct impact on you and your lifestyle because of their willingness to be salty?

* Are you hesitant to be open about your faith? Why or why not?

* What are some ways you can increase your effect on others as you live out your faith in front of your friends?

PRAYER PROMPTS

....

Morning: Pray that you will add seasoning to the world today.

Something like this. . .

> *Dear God, I just want to make an impact for You in the world around me. I don't want to overseason it by being obnoxious, but I want to be a robust offering of Your truth. Help me to know just what to do to be the perfect blend. Amen.*

Afternoon: Pray that someone asks you about your faith.

Something like this. . .

> *Dear God, please let my faith be evident to everyone around me so much so that someone asks me what it's all*

about. Then help me have the words
to say to point them to You. Amen.

Evening: Pray for specific people in your life.
Something like this. . .

Father, I have a whole list of people
who need to know You: (list names).
Please use me as an instrument to
help them find You. Help me to stay
just salty enough that they want to
know You for themselves. Amen.

Day 24

• •

BLAME GAME

• •

*"And why worry about a speck in your
friend's eye when you have a log in your own?
How can you think of saying to your friend,
'Let me help you get rid of that speck in your
eye,' when you can't see past the log in your
own eye? Hypocrite! First get rid of the log
in your own eye; then you will see well
enough to deal with the speck
in your friend's eye."*
MATTHEW 7:3-5 NLT

One of my daughters recently got in a car accident. An oncoming car was driving somewhat erratically at the same time a car was slowing down to turn from her lane. Rather than slow down to avoid plowing into the car in front of her, she panicked and just let the accident happen. She hadn't had her driver's license very long, and she made a very common mistake. She was more worried about what the cars around her were doing than she was about her own driving. It's definitely important to be alert to the behaviors of other drivers, but defensive driving (controlling your own vehicle first) is the best way to avoid a crash.

The same is true in relationships. It's easy to point fingers at other people and the things they are doing wrong while ignoring our own sinful actions. Matthew 7 explains that we need to get ourselves clean before God without worrying about others around us. When we point fingers at them, we're missing the fact that our sin is even greater. We aren't to ignore sin in the world around us, but we are to clean up our own lives before we worry about others.

Once we have truly allowed God to reveal our own issues, and we are positive that our motives are pure, then it is good to help hold our Christian brothers and sisters accountable for their choices. That can only be pure if it's done in love, fully aware that we can fall into the same sin at any time, with the desire to help them see truth and turn from sin.

WHAT'S UP?

* *

* What sinful actions, thoughts, or
  attitudes do you need to confess
  before God?

* Are there any relationships that need
  to be reconciled because you worried
  more about someone else's sin than
  your own?

* Write a script for how you might lov-
  ingly approach someone to help them
  become aware of a sin in their lives.

PRAYER PROMPTS
••••••••••••••••••••••••••••••••

Morning: Pray that God would keep you humble today.

Something like this. . .

> *Dear God, I know that I make*
> *mistakes all the time. Help me to*
> *see where I'm in error rather than*
> *always counting the mistakes of*
> *others. Help me to face my sin with*
> *humility and repentance so I can be*
> *clean before You. Amen.*

Afternoon: Ask God to soften your heart toward others.

Something like this. . .

> *Dear God, please help me be a*
> *loving example of You, not a judge*
> *of others. Give me discernment to*

know when I should speak up and when I should stay quiet. Use my life and my words to draw people to You. Amen.

Evening: Ask God to reveal your sin. Something like this. . .

Father, thank You for Your forgiveness and love. I know I've squandered it in new ways today, ways I don't even realize. Please forgive me for my shortcomings and help me to learn from them so I don't repeat the same mistakes tomorrow. I just want to know You more. Amen.

Day 25

SLOW TO SPEAK

*My dear brothers and sisters, take note of this:
Everyone should be quick to listen, slow
to speak and slow to become angry.*
JAMES 1:19 NIV

Have you ever considered why we have two ears but only one mouth? We girls sure do get the talking done though, don't we? What if we had the opposite—two mouths and one ear? We could argue with ourselves and only hear half of it. Okay, maybe not, but you get my point.

Did God design us that way to make a point? Maybe! The truth is, His intention for us is to listen well and talk much less than we listen. When we listen, we learn, we take in new concepts and ideas, we get a better understanding of another person's heart, and we grow in knowledge of all kinds of things. When we speak, we can't absorb anything, much less learn. And listening is an active skill. To really listen, you have to turn off your train of thought and consider what's being said. You can't be thinking of the next thing you're going to say—that's not real listening.

What that verse from James (quoted above) is saying is to just be patient as you interact with others. Don't be so intent on making your point or being right that you miss an opportunity to share and learn. Hold your tongue. Listen well and think carefully before you speak because words can't be taken back once they're out there. Think of the trouble you could save yourself if you have enough self-control not to speak sharply to your parents or gossip with your friends about someone else.

If you listen twice as much as you talk, you'll save yourself from a heap of problems and you'll be a much better witness for Jesus.

WHAT'S UP?

* *

* Why is listening more important than talking?

* Think of a few times when you spoke before you really heard what the other person was saying and your words got you into a mess.

* What skills do you need to develop to be a better hearer and a slower speaker?

PRAYER PROMPTS

Morning: Pray that God would help you be slow to speak today.

Something like this. . .

> *Dear God, my words often get me into trouble. Please help me guard my tongue today so I can be quick to listen and slow to speak. Help me step back and really consider what people are saying rather than trying so hard to be heard. Amen.*

Afternoon: Ask God to help you repair relationships where your words have done damage.

Something like this. . .

> *Dear God, I'm sorry for hurting people with my words. Would You alert my spirit to anyone I may have hurt*

*with my words and bridge the gap
for reconciliation to happen? Help
me know the words to say to make it
right with them. Amen.*

Evening: Ask Him to help make you known
for your listening skills.

Something like this. . .

*Father, people feel most loved when
they are heard. Help me to be that
person who really listens and hears.
Let that be a trait that I become
known for. May people come to me
because they know I will listen well
and really hear them. Amen.*

Day 26

TAKE HEART

Wait patiently for the LORD. Be brave and courageous. Yes, wait patiently for the LORD.
PSALM 27:14 NLT

COURAGE, n. [L., the heart.] Bravery; intrepidity; that quality of mind which enables men to encounter danger and difficulties with firmness, or without fear or depression of spirits; valor; boldness; resolution. It is a constituent part of fortitude; but fortitude implies patience to bear continued suffering.
– Webster's Dictionary (1828)

Are you nervous about the future? I get it! As a teenager, you're looking ahead to all of life's big issues and important choices. College, career, marriage, family. . .and all of those choices come with big responsibilities. There's a lot of pressure to get it right because the results of the wrong choice can be seemingly catastrophic.

But God calls you to be patient and courageous. Doesn't that sound a little bit like a contradiction? Patience would mean being still and waiting, but courage would imply moving forward no matter the risk. I see it differently though. Courage means facing issues with wisdom and confidence, eager to do it the right way, even if there's a cost or a risk. It means waiting when needed and moving when it's time. It means being open to things that feel confusing or come with new and scary experiences. Courage requires faith, and patience is one way to walk out that faith.

Do these verses not encourage your heart, teen girl? How can we fear what lies before us when God stresses over and over in His Word how He will not fail us or forsake us? Are you dealing with belligerent, unsaved loved ones? What about kids at school who mock your stand? Are you chastised by the lost because you share what God's Word has to say about homosexuality, adultery, or fornication? Do even other believers shake their heads at you for your stand on the King James Bible? Is the battle for the Lord becoming weary? Be of good courage and take heart!

WHAT'S UP?

....

* What are your biggest fears of the future? Make a list of your top 3–5.

* What are some short-term fears? Make a list of those.

* Write a prayer of surrender of those specific fears. Call on your faith to give you the patience and courage you need to face your fears.

PRAYER PROMPTS

Morning: Pray that God would make you confident today.

Something like this. . .

> *Dear God, I trust in You fully.*
> *Please help me to walk boldly today,*
> *confident that You are with me and*
> *guiding me. Give me courage to face*
> *my fears with boldness today. Amen.*

Afternoon: Ask Him to show you how to prepare to face future fears.

Something like this. . .

> *Dear God, You know what's around*
> *the corner, but I don't. Please give me*
> *faith that You've got it all covered*
> *and help me prepare to face whatever*
> *comes. I will wait patiently for You*

*to tell me to act, and then I will be
courageous. Amen.*

Evening: Ask Him to bring a mentor into
your life to show you what courage looks like.
Something like this. . .

*Father, some lessons are best learned
by watching someone else. Would You
bring someone into my life who can
show me what it's like to use godly
courage in the face of hardship or
challenges? And then help me to be
that kind of person when I need to.
Amen.*

Day 27

A BAD RAP

And let us consider how we may spur one
another on toward love and good deeds,
not giving up meeting together, as some
are in the habit of doing, but encouraging
one another—and all the more as
you see the Day approaching.
HEBREWS 10:24-25 NIV

Teenage girls get a bad rap for being moody, hormonal, and negative—at least at home. When I was a teen, people used to tell my mom that I was such a delight—so sunny and warmhearted, such a gentle and sweet spirit. My mom's mouth would drop open as she tried to imagine to whom they were referring.

Surely not the surly, grumpy teenager that lived under her roof! That doesn't sound a bit like you though, does it?

I think back to who I was at that time. I knew everything and couldn't be taught a thing. Especially by my parents. I was closed off to correction and would argue the sky was yellow if it meant I could be right. I wish I hadn't been that way though. I wish I'd opened my mind to learn from others so I could have avoided a lot of mistakes along the way.

God wants you to be teachable, open to correction, and moldable. How else can He help you become the woman He wants you to be? Sometimes the moodiness that comes with being a teenager is a real biological thing because of the hormonal shifts in your body, but that doesn't mean it's okay to be disrespectful at home. Look to Jesus for help with your attitude in those times.

Those parents of mine? You know, the ones who didn't know anything? Yeah, turns out they were pretty smart after all. There's still time for you, so take advantage of the opportunity you have to learn from yours.

WHAT'S UP?

....

* Think of some times when you were sure you were right but discovered later that you weren't.

* What are some examples of good pieces of advice you've gotten from other people?

* What can you do when you feel moody and closed off?

PRAYER PROMPTS

•••••••••••••••••••••••••••••

Morning: Pray that God would make you open today.

Something like this...

> *Dear God, please help me keep my mind open to leadership and correction today. Remind me that it's in my best interest to learn because I don't know everything. Help me to be grateful for the people who want to help me grow. Amen.*

Afternoon: Ask God to teach you something new.

Something like this...

> *Dear God, may all my correction and growth start with You. I want everything You have for me. So what*

new thing do You have for me today?
Amen.

Evening: Ask for forgiveness if you messed up.
Something like this. . .

Father, I lost it with my parents
today. I'm sorry to You and to them
that I didn't control my tongue and
my attitude. Please help me have
better self-control tomorrow. Amen.

Day 28

MONEY TALKS

Humility is the fear of the LORD;
its wages are riches and
honor and life.
PROVERBS 22:4 NIV

Talking about money is so boring! And that is especially true when you're a teenager and probably don't have a ton of it. But if you consider financial goals now, you'll be so far ahead of your peers and closer to financial freedom and success.

Clothes, electronics, cars, and then one day, a house. Those are all material possessions that can easily suck us into overspending. But debt is no fun long-term. Every item you buy on credit just stacks up month to month, until you're actually working just to pay rent on a pile of debt that never goes down. Many people your age have launched their financial habits with credit card debt. It compounded for a few months or years, and then they found themselves twenty-eight years old and still living with Mom and Dad, unable to support themselves because they owe too much money. Just think about that. If you can own that concept now, before the first credit card offer shows up in your mailbox with all its temptation, you'll make far better decisions than most of your peers.

If you want to achieve more in life, have the ability to be generous toward others, and still have nice things like a car and house, you've got to start your financial plan now. It takes a lot of planning and intentional behaviors to get to where you want to be. Setting up financial goals and making a plan to get there isn't easy. It takes some work and a lot of sacrifice.

But God wants you to steward (use wisely and take care of) the blessings He gives you, and that starts with your financial habits.

WHAT'S UP?

....

* Where do you see yourself in ten years? How about twenty? Describe those scenarios.

* What are your financial goals?

* What steps can you begin to take now to help make those goals a reality?

PRAYER PROMPTS

• •

Morning: Pray that God would give you financial wisdom today.

Something like this. . .

> *Dear God, thank You for the finances*
> *You've entrusted to me. Please help*
> *me to make wise financial choices*
> *today and every day so I can use*
> *them for Your glory. Amen.*

Afternoon: Ask God to help you establish sound financial principles.

Something like this. . .

> *Dear God, I want to be smart*
> *about my money. Would You help*
> *me set up a budget and give me the*
> *resolve to avoid credit card debt?*
> *Help me stay the course with the*

big picture in mind. Amen.

Evening: Ask Him to bless you for the right reasons.

Something like this. . .

> *Father, I want to be a good steward of money. I want to be generous and open, not materialistic and entitled. Please bless me financially so I can bless others and help more people know You. Amen.*

Day 29

TWENTY-ONE DAYS

● ●

*People ruin their lives by their own
foolishness and then are angry at the LORD.*
PROVERBS 19:3 NLT

Have you ever thought about the habits
you already have? You probably have tons
of them. Some bad habits are things like
staying up too late, biting your fingernails,
or cracking your knuckles. Others are bigger things like eating too much fast food,
watching too much television, and looking
at your phone too much. Some good habits
might be things like reading your Bible every
morning before school, exercising regularly,

or eating plenty of fruits and vegetables.

Bad habits can be really hard to stop. They have become a normal part of your day and you probably do them mindlessly. To break a habit, you first have to decide to do it. Then you need to pay close attention to when and why you do the thing you need to stop. You can ask God to help you notice it so you can stop it. Then find a creative replacement for the habit. For example, if your bad habit is eating too much fast food, find something healthy on the menu so you can replace the bad choice with a better one.

At the same time you want to break some bad habits, you might want to pick up some good ones. They say it takes twenty-one days of repetition to instill a habit. So whatever it is you decide you want to start, you need to do it every day for three weeks before it becomes a natural part of your life. Just like an athlete has to train with repetition until their sport becomes second nature to them, good habits require diligence and effort. Good habits don't show up in your life by accident; they are gained with lots of hard work and discipline.

WHAT'S UP?

* *

* Make a list of five bad habits you'd like to break.

* Using the list you wrote above, what is a creative replacement you can do for each one?

* Now think of one or two good habits you want to bring into your life. How can you start those actions?

PRAYER PROMPTS

Morning: Pray that God would help you see the bad habits you need to break.

Something like this. . .

> *Dear God, I didn't even know I had bad habits. Would You please help me see when I actually act on my bad habits so I can try to stop? Amen.*

Afternoon: Ask God to help you find creative replacements.

Something like this. . .

> *Dear God, bad habits are really hard to break. Please help me replace the bad things I'm doing with something good or fun. Help me see the value in doing things better every day. Amen.*

Evening: Ask Him to point out some good habits you can begin to instill in your life.

Something like this. . .

> *Father, now that I'm facing and
> dealing with my bad habits, would
> You show me some good ones I
> already have and help me pick up
> a few more good things in my life?
> Thank You for teaching me new
> things every day. Amen.*

Day 30

NEVER TOO YOUNG

*Don't let anyone look down on you because
you are young, but set an example for
the believers in speech, in conduct,
in love, in faith and in purity.*
1 TIMOTHY 4:12 NIV

History tells us that Timothy was in his early twenties when Paul told him (above) not to let people look down on him for being young, but to show them that age didn't matter when God wanted him to do something. Timothy definitely took that advice by remaining sold out and committed to spreading the Gospel. The records of his words and actions speak for themselves.

When I was fifteen, I worked as a youth counselor at the local crisis pregnancy center. I had developed a passion for the pro-life message from an early age, and I really wanted to serve in that arena somehow. I approached someone I knew who worked at the center as a counselor and asked her if they had any jobs I could do. I figured they'd have me fold baby clothes or clean the facility. But they actually let me be a counselor. They'd never had someone as young as I was do that, but they decided to give it a try because they thought I could probably relate to the teenagers better than some of the older counselors. It was an amazing experience! I got to talk to young girls who were dealing with a scary surprise pregnancy, and I even got to go with a couple of them to help them tell their parents that they were pregnant. I loved that I could reach them with practical and spiritual help—even though I was so young!

God made us each different, so your

interests and passions might look very different than mine. That's awesome! You can start now to find your place in ministry and begin to make a difference in people's lives no matter how old you are.

WHAT'S UP?

* *

* What passions do you have? What messages get you really excited that you want to share with others?

* How can you begin to step into that area of ministry? Think of a few ideas.

* Who can help you with that? Think of people like ministry leaders at church, community leaders, and people who are already doing what you'd like to do.

PRAYER PROMPTS

Morning: Pray that God would begin to open your eyes to His plan for you.

Something like this. . .

> *Dear God, thank You for creating*
> *me to have a unique purpose in the*
> *kingdom, and I believe that there's*
> *work for me to do. Please help me to*
> *see where You'd have me start to do*
> *Your work. Amen.*

Afternoon: Ask God to open doors for you.

Something like this. . .

> *Dear God, now that I know You*
> *have a plan for me even now, I'm so*
> *excited to get started. Would You open*
> *doors and help me make connections*
> *that would move me along? Thank*

*You for building this passion within
me. Amen.*

Evening: Pray for the people you will reach
out to.

Something like this. . .

*Father, as I serve You throughout
my life, I'm sure I will encounter all
sorts of people. Would You go before
me on the path and pave the way
that they would welcome my help
and my words? Give me the words
that would open people's eyes to You.
I want to be about You. Amen.*

Scripture Index

About the Author

A mom of six, including triplets, **Nicole O'Dell** is a multi-published author in both inspirational fiction and nonfiction. Her passion is to bridge the gap between parents and teens, and she writes with conviction and authenticity from her own experiences.

You'll Love These...

The Prayer Map for Teens
This unique prayer journal is an engaging and creative way for you to understand the importance and experience the power of prayer. Each page features a fun, 2-color design that guides you to write out specific thoughts, ideas, and lists. . .which then creates a specific "map" to follow as you talk to God.

Spiral Bound / 978-1-68322-556-0 / $7.99

3-Minute Devotions for Teen Girls
Girls will find just the wisdom and encouragement they need in *3-Minute Devotions for Teen Girls*. This practical devotional packs a powerful dose of inspiration into 3 short minutes. Minute 1: scripture to meditate on. Minute 2: a just-right-sized devotional reading. Minute 3: a prayer to jump-start a conversation with God.

Paperback / 978-1-63058-856-4 / $4.99

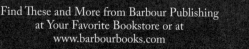

Find These and More from Barbour Publishing
at Your Favorite Bookstore or at
www.barbourbooks.com

BARBOUR
PUBLISHING